Compact Schülerhilfen

Englisch

Diktat

5./6. Klasse

Helmut Streifinger

Compact Verlag

Redaktion: Petra Bachmann, Thomas Martin
Umschlaggestaltung: Sabine Jantzen
Printed in Germany
ISBN 3-8174-7347-8
7373471

INHALT

Wie du mit diesem Buch lernen kannst! *5*

A. Rechtschreibung *7*

1. Groß- und Kleinschreibung **8**

1.1 Das Pronomen *I* 8
1.2 Die Namen von Personen, Familienangehörigen und Firmen 8
1.3 Die Namen von Städten, Ländern, ihren Bewohnern und die davon abgeleiteten Adjektive 9
1.4 Die Namen von Straßen, Plätzen, Gebäuden und Gewässern 9
1.5 Die Namen von Feiertagen, Monaten und Tagen 9

2. Die Verdoppelungsregel **12**

2.1 Verformen auf *-ing* und *-ed* 12
2.2 Adjektive in der Steigerungsform 13

3. Die Veränderung von *-y* **16**

3.1 Substantive 16
3.2 Verben 16
3.3 Adjektive und Adverbien 18

4. Wegfall des stummen *-e* **21**

4.1 Verben 21
4.2 Adjektive 22
4.2.1 Steigerung 22
4.2.2 Bildung des Adverbs 23

5. Wörter mit den Endungen *-o* und *-f* **25**

6. *-s* am Wortende **27**

7. Unregelmäßige Verben **30**

8. Gleichlautende Wörter und Formen (Homophone) **36**

9. Ähnlichlautende Wörter 39

10. Schwierige Wörter 42

B. Diktatsammlung 46

1. Diktate für die Anfangsstufe 47

2. Diktate für das erste Lernjahr 62

3. Diktate für das zweite Lernjahr - Stufe 1 72

4. Diktate für das zweite Lernjahr - Stufe 2 84

C. *Lösungen* *94*

Wie du mit diesem Buch lernen kannst!

Diktate gehören von Anfang an zum Englischlernen, und sie sind ein wichtiger Bestandteil der Schulaufgaben bis in die Mittelstufe. Sicherheit im Diktat ist aber auch die Voraussetzung für den Erfolg in der Nacherzählung in der 9. bis 11. Klasse und natürlich dafür, daß wir verstehen, was uns ein Gast aus London oder ein Tourist aus Amerika sagen will.

Meist sind es drei Gründe, warum beim Diktat Fehler passieren: Entweder du verstehst das Wort nicht, oder du beherrschst seine Rechtschreibung nicht, oder du verwechselst es mit einem ähnlichen Wort.
Dieses Buch möchte dir helfen, durch Lernen und Üben sicher zu werden. Im ersten Teil geht es um Rechtschreibregeln. Präge dir die Merksätze ein und überprüfe gleich mit den Aufgaben dein Wissen. Der zweite Teil bietet viele Diktate, die nach Schwierigkeitsstufen geordnet sind. Eine genaue Anleitung findest du am Anfang von Teil B.

Die Auswertung der Übungsdiktate zeigt dir deine persönlichen Fehlerquellen. Anhand der entsprechenden Regeln und Übungen kannst du deine Schwachstellen gezielt trainieren. Wenn du danach die Diktate wiederholst und deine Fehler vergleichst, erkennst du deinen Lernerfolg.

Übrigens hilft dir auch unser Bär beim Zurechtfinden; was die Buchstaben bedeuten, die er dir zeigt, siehst du auf der nächsten Seite.

Und nun viel Spaß und Erfolg beim Englischlernen!

Helmut Streifinger

Der Bär hilft dir, dich zurechtzufinden:

= Beispiel: Hier findest du wichtige Lernbeispiele, die du dir mit der Regel zusammen einprägen solltest.

= Aufgaben: Schreibe die Lösungen zu den Übungen in dein Arbeitsheft – nicht ins Buch.

= Test: Diese Übungsdiktate fassen mehrere Lernthemen zusammen. So kannst du kontrollieren, ob du den Stoff auch wirklich beherschst. Wenn nicht, dann bearbeite das betreffende Kapitel noch einmal.

Wichtige Regeln, die du dir einprägen solltest, sind rot markiert.

A. RECHTSCHREIBUNG

In diesem Kapitel findest du alle Rechtschreibregeln, die für deine ersten englischen Diktate wichtig sind. Das Kapitel ist so aufgebaut, daß du es unterrichtsbegleitend als zusätzliche Erläuterung benutzen kannst oder selbständig damit arbeitest, indem du Stück für Stück lernst und übst. Außerdem kannst du hier noch einmal die Regeln nachschlagen, wenn du bei der Arbeit im Teil B deine Fehler gezielt verbessern willst.

Achte beim Lernen darauf, daß du dir zuerst die Regeln und Beispiele einprägst, sie dann im Kopf wiederholst und erst dann die Aufgaben löst und Testdiktate schreibst. Vergleiche nach Abschluß der Arbeit dein Ergebnis mit den angegebenen Lösungen im Teil C und mit den Regeln.
Sicher kennst du die wichtigsten Bezeichnungen der Grammatik und der Zeichensetzung im Deutschen und Englischen. Präge sie dir nochmals gut ein:

Artikel	Begleiter	article
Substantiv	Hauptwort	noun
Singular	Einzahl	singular
Plural	Mehrzahl	plural
Verb	Zeitwort	verb
Hilfsverb	Hilfszeitwort	auxiliary
Infinitiv	Grundform	infinitive
Adjektiv	Eigenschaftswort	adjective
Adverb	Umstandswort	adverb
Personalpronomen	persönliches Fürwort	personal pronoun
Possessivpronomen	besitzanzeigendes Fürwort	possessive pronoun
–	Punkt	full stop
–	Komma	comma
Semikolon	Strichpunkt	semicolon
–	Doppelpunkt	colon
–	Fragezeichen	question mark
–	Ausrufezeichen	exclamation mark
–	Anführungsstriche	quotation marks

1. Groß- und Kleinschreibung

Anders als im Deutschen werden Substantive im Englischen grundsätzlich klein geschrieben, wenn sie nicht am Satzanfang stehen. Von dieser Regel gibt es einige Ausnahmen, die du dir merken solltest:

1.1 Das Pronomen *I*

Das Pronomen ***I*** wird immer groß geschrieben:

Peter and **I** are good friends.

Beachte, daß alle anderen Pronomen klein geschrieben werden:
Thank **you** for your letter.

1.2 Die Namen von Personen, Familienangehörigen und Firmen

Groß geschrieben werden auch die Namen von Personen, Familienangehörigen und Firmen:

Mr Brown is talking to **U**ncle **B**en.
Mary and **T**om are good friends.
We fly with **B**ritish **A**irways.

Wird dagegen nur das reine Verwandtschaftsverhältnis, meist mit Possessivpronomen my, your, his etc., bezeichnet, wird die Kleinschreibung verwendet:

My **u**ncle and my three **b**rothers are fishing at the lake.
His **f**ather is a doctor.
Your little **s**ister is eating the whole cake!

1.3 Die Namen von Städten, Ländern, ihren Bewohnern und die davon abgeleiteten Adjektive

Ebenfalls groß schreiben mußt du Städte- und Ländernamen, die Nationalitätsbezeichnungen und die sich davon ableitenden Adjektive:

In the summer we go to **S**cotland.
The people who live there are **B**ritish.
My father drives an **A**merican car.
We live in **L**ondon.
He speaks **E**nglish, **I**talian, and **S**panish.

1.4 Die Namen von Straßen, Plätzen, Gebäuden und Gewässern

Grundsätzlich groß geschrieben werden die Namen von Straßen, Plätzen, Gebäuden und Gewässern:

You will find a bakery in **S**mith **S**treet.
After you have seen the **T**ower of **L**ondon you must visit the **H**ouses of **P**arliament and **B**ig **B**en. These buildings are all on the **T**hames.

Gebäude, Wege und Gewässer als solche hingegen mußt du klein schreiben:

The **h**ouse is at the end of the **s**treet near the **l**ake.
The **t**ower of the **c**hurch is very old.

1.5 Die Namen von Feiertagen, Monaten und Tagen

Feiertage, Monate und Wochentage werden immer groß geschrieben:

Uncle Bert wants to see us at **E**aster.
Daddy's birthday is in **J**une.
The party is on **M**onday.

Allgemeine Zeitbezeichnungen hingegen werden klein geschrieben:

John will be fifteen next **m**onth.
We still have five **m**inutes time. It's just five **o'c**lock.
Every **y**ear we go to Ireland.

Aufgabe 1: Setze die Anfangsbuchstaben ein.

1. In .ermany school starts in .ugust or in the first .eeks of .eptember.
2. The .chool of my friend .eter is a modern building in .mith .treet in .ondon.
3. He's got at two .eeks' holiday at .hristmas.
4. In his class there are children from .taly and .merica.
5. His friend .edro is .panish.
6. In the .ummer he visits him at his .ome in .arcelona.
7. .eter's .ather works for .ritish .irways.
8. So he says, "One day I can fly with .addy!"
9. His mother is .talian.
10. Her parents live in a small .own in Southern .taly.
11. Sometimes they come to .ngland.
12. Then Peter shows them interesting .laces and .treets in .ondon.
13. At .uckingham .alace they see .ueen .lizabeth's guards.

Aufgabe 2: Setze die Anfangsbuchstaben ein.

1. .ony and .ary are planning a holiday in .cotland.
2. They know that .cottish people are friendly and helpful.
3. Their .ather has a .rother in .dinburgh, so they can stay there near the .astle.
4. They are asking their .other lots of questions, "Look, .ummy, can we take our new pullover from .merica with us?"
5. At the railway station in .dinburgh they see their .ncle first: "Oh look, there's .ncle Kevin, and .unt Lora, too!
6. Now they are driving to the house in .astle .oad at the end of the town.
7. They are going to stay over .aster.
8. They have got a plan for every .ay of the .eek.
9. On .onday they want to see the old .astle of the .cottish kings.

10. On .ednesday there is a concert by an .nglish orchestra.
11. At the .eekend they plan to go to the coast.
12. At the end of their holiday they fly home with .ritish .irways.
13. Their plane leaves from .dinburgh airport on .aturday, 22nd .pril.
14. Perhaps the stewardess is from .ndia or .ustralia.

Übe die Groß- und Kleinschreibung mit den folgenden zwei Diktaten:

Visitors from Germany

Sandra and Barbara are German girls. They are in England for their summer holidays. It's August, but the days are not as hot as in Italy. The girls can sleep in their aunt's house. Aunt Mary and Uncle Tom have a fine home near London with a big garden and Fluffy, the dog. When they go shopping in Station Road, they often see British children. On Monday afternoon their uncle takes them to the swimming pool. It's in the same street as the school. The next weekend they want to go to London. On Saturday there is a lot of traffic, so it's good to go on Sunday. They can take a red bus and see the town from a seat at the top.

Giving a party

Mr Hill is Barbara's father. The Hills have got a nice house in Oak Street. Barbara is asking her mother about the party on Friday, "Look, Mum, can I bring Tom to the party? His father is English and his mother is German. They live in Germany and are now here for their Easter holidays." Barbara and her sister Kate are shopping in London Road, two streets away from their house. They see Mr Clean, Kate's English teacher, "Good afternoon, Mr Clean. Can you come to our party on Friday?" "Oh thank you very much. I can bring a Beatles' record!"

2. Die Verdoppelungsregel

2.1 Verbformen auf *-ing* und *-ed*

Endet ein Verb im Infinitiv auf einen Konsonanten (*b,d,g,m,n,p,t*), so wird dieser vor *-ing* und *-ed* verdoppelt, wenn vor ihm ein einfacher, kurzer Vokal steht. Bei mehrsilbigen Verben muß diese letzte Silbe betont sein:

get	-	ge**tt**ing	begin	-	begi**nn**ing
swim	-	swi**mm**ing	stop	-	sto**pp**ing

Keine Verdoppelung finden wir also z.B. bei

cl**ea**ning	(zwei Vokale vor dem n!)
wa**l**king	(zwei Endkonsonanten!
co**m**ing	(m steht nicht am Ende von come!)
happening	(die letzte Silbe ist nicht betont!)
thr**ow**ing	(o ist lang, w ist stumm!)

Einen Sonderfall stellt das *l* dar. Es wird auch nach unbetontem Vokal verdoppelt:

Many people are now trave**ll**ing to Britain.

Aufgabe 3: Setze die Verbformen ein.

1. I am just (begin) to learn English.
2. I am (read) the text and (write) it.
3. My father is (sit) in the garden and (feed) the cat.
4. Our dog is (bark) and (look) at the cat.
5. Jim and Sally are (swim) in the pool and (shout).
6. Baby Michael is (sleep) upstairs and (feel) happy.
7. My brother is (listen) to pop music and (eat) a banana.
8. He is (wait) for his girlfriend because they are (go) to see a film tonight.
9. Now Mother is (cook) dinner in the kitchen
10. We are (wait) because we are very hungry.
11. The baby is (help) her with the noodles: he is (throw) them on the floor.
12. Our cat is (put) the noodles in its basket now.
13. Of course Mother is (shout) at Michael and the cat!

Aufgabe 4: Setze die richtigen Verbformen ein.

1. Last week we were (sit) together and (make) plans for our holidays.
2. It was (rain) and the raindrops were (hit) against the window.
3. Suddenly John noticed that the door bell was (ring).
4. He (shout), (stand) up and (open) the door.
5. We all (stop) (talk) and (look) at the door.
6. A man was (offer) John some magazines.
7. John (listen) to the man for some time, but then (want) to shut the door.
8. While he was (shut) the door, the man (look) angry.
9. He said, “I (travel) around and never sell anything!”
10. John (wait) a minute and then (ask) him about the magazines.
11. The man (show) him three different journals.
12. One (look) interesting and (offer) help with car repairs.
13. The other two (help) people repair things in the house.
14. In the end John (order = bestellen) a magazine for one year.

2.2 Adjektive in der Steigerungsform

Bei der Steigerung von Adjektiven wird der Endkonsonant nach **kurzem** und **betontem** Vokal verdoppelt, wenn die Steigerungsendungen *-er* und *-est* folgen:

The baby has got a temperature; his head is ho**tt**er than it was yesterday.
This is the bi**gg**est apple of all.

Keine Verdoppelung finden wir, wenn
- vor dem Endkonsonanten zwei Vokale stehen,
- wenn das Adjektiv auf zwei oder mehr Konsonanten endet,
- das Adjektiv auf einen Vokal endet
- oder bei einem mehrsilbigen Adjektiv die Betonung nicht auf der Endsilbe liegt:

These apples are chea**p**er.	(zwei Vokale vor dem p!)
Tom has got the bri**ght**est ideas.	(3 Endkonsonanten!)
This field is larger than that field.	(g ist nicht Endlaut!)
Francis is cleverer than Alison.	(Endsilbe ist nicht betont!)

Merke dir als Faustregel die **„sitting - Regel":**
Der Endkonsonant wird nach kurzem betontem Vokal verdoppelt.

Aufgabe 5: Setze jeweils die 2. und 3. Steigerungsform ein.

1. Apples are ... than oranges, but potatoes are ... .(cheap)
2. Glasgow is ... than Colchester, but London is the ... city in Britain. (big)
3. In Italy it's ... than in Britain, but Sudan is certainly the ... country. (hot)
4. In Iceland it's ... than in Spain, but Alaska is certainly the ... country. (cold)
5. Peter is perhaps ... than Mary, but Sandra is the ... of all. (clever)
6. Holland is ... than Germany, but the Sahara is ... . (flat)
7. My teeth are ... than my brother's, but a film star has certainly the ... teeth. (clean)
8. If dogs eat sausages, they get ... than if they eat meat, but they become ... if they aren't walked enough. (fat)
9. 90-year-old Uncle Ben is ... than 75-year-old Aunt Gwendolyn; but Grandma is the ... . She is 95. (old)
10. Red is ... than black, but white is ... . (light)
11. November is a ... month than February, but December is the ... of these three. (long)
12. Germany is ... than Belgium, but the U.S.A. is the ... country. (large)
13. My hair is ... than yours, but Mike's hair is ... . (short)

Der folgende **„magische Satz"** wird dir im ersten Teil des Buches immer wieder begegnen. In ihm findest du, als kleine Eselsbrücke, jeweils auf ein Wort verkürzt, alle Regeln wieder, die behandelt werden. Sobald die Regel erklärt worden ist, wird das entsprechende Wort fett gedruckt erscheinen:

Happily **sitting** on the potatoes the wolves were giving their parties.

Übe die Steigerungsformen mit den folgenden zwei Diktaten:

An apple for the dog

Tom is sitting behind David. Look, he's eating and Mr Green is looking at him. The apple is bigger than a tomato, but greener than grass.
Tom, stop doing that!
Now Tom is putting the apple in his school bag. At home his apple is brown and flatter than a sandwich. His books are all dirty. Fluffy, the dog, is waiting at the door. Now Tom is cleaning his books and the dog is beginning to eat the old apple.
Oh Tom, you're not the cleverest boy!

The stone

Last night I was sleeping deeply in my bed. I was dreaming that I travelled across the sea. Suddenly a stone hit my bedroom window. In a moment I was sitting up. My face was hotter than before. In the street a dog was barking and a man was shouting. I opened the window and looked down. A boy was running away. For some minutes I listened and waited. Nothing happened, so I returned to my bed.
The next morning, when I was beginning to remember the night, I quickly went into the garden and found the stone. It was not bigger than a mouse, but much flatter.
I think it was not the boy's brightest idea to throw it at the house.

2. Lernjahr

3. Die Veränderung von -y

3.1 Substantive

Substantive, die auf **Konsonant + *y*** enden, bilden den Plural auf *-ies:*

Peter has a lot of interesting hobb**ies**.(hobby)
Uncle Tom always knows fine stor**ies**.(story)
Scotland and Ireland are beautiful countr**ies**.(country)

Steht im Singular jedoch ein **Vokal vor** dem ***y***, bleibt es auch im Plural erhalten:

Every year we spend our holida**ys** in Bath.

Aufgabe 6: Setze die Substantive in den Plural.

1. Many (family) spend their (holiday) in other (country).
2. There are many (way) to travel.
3. When they fly to Gibraltar, they can find the last wild (monkey) in Europe.
4. They buy some souvenirs: (toy) for the (baby), nice drinks for (party), things for their friends' (hobby).
5. Back home again, they tell their friends about hotels with nice (balcony) in beautiful (city).
6. They know a lot of (story).

3.2 Verben

Verben, die auf **Konsonant + *y*** enden, bilden die 3. Person Singular auf *-ies* und das Simple Past auf *-ied*:

Mummy always dr**ies** the washing in the sun.
Fluffy is a nice dog; if I hurry, he hurr**ies**, too.
He also carr**ies** Daddy's newspaper.

Steht in der Grundform des Verbs jedoch ein **Vokal vor** dem ***y***, bleibt es in den anderen Formen erhalten:

He often says that he never bu**ys** any sweets.

Beachte: Um das Aufeinandertreffen von *ii* zu vermeiden, bleibt das *y* vor *-ing* erhalten.

Look, Mum is dr**yi**ng the washing.
Fluffy is hurr**yi**ng after a bird.
He is carr**yi**ng Daddy's paper.

Aus diesem Grund bilden sogar Verben, die auf *-ie* enden, die *-ing*-Form mit *y*.

So many people d**ie** in accidents. The man was d**yi**ng on the road.
People should not l**ie** in the sun too long. Look at the beach, some have been l**yi**ng there the whole day.

Ein Wort, das sich an keine Regel halten will, ist "to ski":
In winter we were **skiing** in Wales.

Merke dir als Faustregel die **„parties - Regel"**:
Nach Konsonanten wird *y* zu *ie*.

Aufgabe 7: Setze die richtigen Verbformen ein.

1. Kevin is (ski) in the Austrian mountains.
2. Now he is (buy) a one-day ticket for the lifts.
3. Look, he is (hurry) to the ski lift.
4. He is (carry) his skis on his shoulders.
5. A lady is (try) to get into the lift, too.
6. First she (try) to push him away, and now she is (lie) on the ground because she hasn't seen the steps.
7. Kevin (say), "Oh sorry, Madam, and helps her into the lift.
8. There the lady is afraid and (cry), "Oh dear, I'm (play) with my life!"
9. Kevin (say) to her, "When somebody (fly) in a plane, he may be more afraid."
10. But the lady shouts, "Oh help me, I'm (die) of fear!"

Aufgabe 8: Setze die richtigen Verbformen ein.

1. Yesterday Tom wanted to buy a budgie. While he was (pay), the bird (try) to climb out of the box.
2. It got out and was soon (fly) around in the shop.
3. While Tom was (hurry) to the door and (try) to keep it shut, the budgie was (play) with the goldfish in the tank.
4. Tom (worry) a lot, but suddenly the bird returned to its box for food.
5. Tom was happy and (carry) the bird home.
6. Oh look, the budgie is (lie) on the floor.
7. It is (die), because the cat (play) with it!
8. My mother is (carry) it into the garden.
9. Dad is (bury = begraben) it under the tree now.

Wiederhole den „magischen Satz":

Happily **sitting** on the potatoes the wolves were giving their **parties.**

3.3 Adjektive und Adverbien

Zweisilbige Adjektive auf **Konsonant + *y*** bilden die Steigerungsformen auf -ier und -iest:

lucky - luck**ier** - luck**iest**
easy - eas**ier** - eas**iest**
lively - livel**ier** - livel**iest**

Steht jedoch ein **Vokal vor** dem ***y***, bleibt es auch in den Steigerungsformen erhalten:

grey - gre**yer** - gre**yest**

Bei der Adverbform wird das *y* ebenfalls zu *i*.

lucky - luckily
easy - easily

Merke dir als Faustregel die **„happily - Regel"**:
y wird zu *i*, wenn davor ein Konsonant steht.

Aufgabe 9: Setze die 2. und 3. Steigerungsform ein.

1. Bus drivers must get up ... than school children, but bakers must start ... of all. (early)
2. On the boat trip Jim was sick. His face was ... than the clouds, but Peter's nose was ... of all. (grey)
3. Little Jimmy's clothes were ... than Tom's, but Sarah's dress was full of ice-cream: it was ... . (dirty)
4. Tom is a great eater: he is always ... than the others, but the ... of all is Garfield, our cat! (hungry)
5. Are girls ... than boys? Certainly all children are not the ... people in a family. (tidy)
6. Cars are ... than bikes, but the ... are motor bikes. (noisy)
7. Riding a horse is ... than riding a camel, but riding a bike is ... . (easy)
8. My joke was ... than yours, but Henry's was the ... of all. (funny)
9. By day cats are always ... than dogs, but our Garfield is the ... animal in the world. (lazy)
10. Girls are certainly not ... than boys; if you think they are, you are the ... of all children. (silly)
11. Managers are ... than holiday makers; but the ... of all are mothers with school children. (busy)
12. If you win 1000 pounds in a lottery, you are ... than other people; but if you are never ill, you are the ... person in the world. (lucky)

Wiederhole den „magischen Satz":

Happily sitting on the potatoes the wolves were giving their **parties**.

Aufgabe 10: Verwandle die folgenden Adjektive in Adverbien und setze sie in den richtigen Satz ein.

lucky - busy- easy- happy - lazy - crazy - hungry - noisy

1. After a long night the wolves were ... eating the meat.
2. They could ... bite it with their strong teeth.

3. They were chewing (to chew = kauen) so ... that everybody could hear it.
4. The little ones were ... trying to get their pieces.
5. ... they got some from their mothers.
6. So some were ... playing with what they had, others were ... fighting with other young ones.
7. After the meal they were all ... lying under a tree.

Und nun zwei Diktate zu der Veränderung von *y*:

Life on a farm

This is Tom. He must get up for school earlier than other pupils because he lives on a farm. Sometimes the roads are dirtier than the roads in the town, but in the afternoon he is happier than his friends. He can see the funniest things on the farm: two rabbits are crazily fighting, a cat is tidily sitting in the chair, the dog is sleeping lazily in its house. In the town it's noisier and not so much fun when everyone is trying to get home and worrying about shopping quickly. In the evening Tom often lies in bed and thinks he is luckier than many other children.

Our hamster

Last week Sandra got a hamster. She carried it home from the pet shop. In the evening her new little friend was busily trying to fill its house with soft things. Then the girl played with it. The hamster tried to climb up on her right arm. Next morning, when the animal was lazily lying in its house, Sandra went to buy some toys for it. She stayed away quite a long time.
Now she is so busy with her pet that she has no time for other hobbies or parties.

4. Wegfall des stummen -e

4.1 Verben

Das **stumme *-e*** am Wortende nach einem Konsonanten fällt vor *-ing* und *-ed* weg:

come - com**ing**
believe - believ**ing** - believ**ed**
pronounce - pronounc**ing** - pronounc**ed**

Steht am Wortende jedoch ein Doppel *-e*, bleibt es vor *-ing* erhalten:

agr**ee** - agr**ee**ing - agr**eed**

Merke dir als Faustregel die **„giving - Regel"**:
Das stumme End *-e* entfällt vor *-ing*

Aufgabe 11: -ing oder *-ed*? Setze die richtige Verbform ein.

1. The sun was (shine) when Mr Hill (move) towards his house.
2. He (imagine) a quiet evening with his family and (hope) to find them inside.
3. But he had no keys (=Schlüssel). He (suppose) they were still in his office. So he (use) the bell.
4. Nobody opened the door. So he (decide) to go to the back garden, but what did he see there?
5. The children were (have) a party and (ride) around the swimming-pool on their bikes.
6. "Hi Dad, come and have a piece of cake!" Well, he (agree)!
7. Later some girls were (argue) about the music.
8. They (hate) the rhythm and the sound of it.
9. They said, "You are (dance) like crazy elephants to this music!"
10. Really, the boys were (move) around quite funnily.
11. After some time they all were (lose) interest in the dance.
12. Slowly the party was (come) to an end.

13. On their way home some (use) the street over the hill. So they (save) time.
14. At midnight Mrs Brown (phone) Mr Hill because Doris was not at home.
15. She said, “I’m (become) quite afraid!”
16. But at that moment she heard that the girl was (use) the back door to enter the house.

Aufgabe 12: Bilde die Normalform und die Verlaufsform (*-ing*-Form) der Gegenwart von den Verben in Klammern.

1. John normally never ... ; but now he ... in a loud voice. (argue)
2. Betty always ... English correctly; but today she ... every word wrongly. (pronounce)
3. Ken never ... toothpaste; but now he ... it because he has to go to the dentist’s. (use)
4. Father ... the number 34 bus to get to work; but today he ... his car because there is a strike. (take)
5. Aunt Cathy never ... us, but today she ... me because it’s my birthday. (phone)

Wiederhole nochmals den „magischen Satz“:

Happily sitting on the potatoes the wolves were **giving** their **parties.**

4.2 Adjektive

4.2.1 Steigerung

Zweisilbige Adjektive auf **Konsonant + *e*** hängen bei der Steigerung nur *-r* bzw. *-est* an:

lat**e** - late**r** - late**st**
nic**e** - nice**r** - nice**st**
larg**e** - large**r** - large**st**

4.2.2 Bildung des Adverbs

Bei **Adjektiven auf** ***-le*** schreiben wir bei der Adverbform statt dem stummen *-e* ein *-y*:

comfortab**le** - comfortab**ly**
terrib**le** - terrib**ly**

Bei allen **Adjektiven**, die **auf** ***-e*** enden, bleibt das *-e* in der Adverbform erhalten:

expensi**ve** - expensiv**ely**
sa**fe** - saf**ely**

Ein Sonderfall stellt das Wort *true* dar: true - truly (wahr, echt - in Wirklichkeit)

Aufgabe 13: Setze ein Adjektiv in der 2. oder 3. Steigerungsform oder ein Adverb ein.

1. Princess Diana is a rich woman. She has the (fine) dresses and the (nice) shoes of all ladies.
2. She buys them (expensive) in Italy or Spain.
3. The newspaper stories about her are (large) than those about politics.
4. But in Germany we read them (late) than the British people. What a pity!
5. But the reports are often (nice) here than in England.
6. Of course, some journalists don't talk (nice) about her.
7. Her cars must be (safe) than those of normal people.
8. The Queen has got the (safe) car of all, a Rolls Royce.
9. Do you know the (late) story about Windsor Castle?
10. There was a fire there in 1992; this was the (large) fire for a long time.
11. It was really the (huge) fire in the town of Windsor.

Hast du dir die Regeln gut eingeprägt? Dann überprüfe dein Wissen mit den folgenden zwei Diktaten:

Peter's birthday

The Browns are giving a birthday party for Peter. Lots of friends are coming, and his aunt is coming by, too. For Peter it's a terribly exciting day, and his guests are bringing larger and nicer presents than last year. He decided to invite his teacher, too, and his friends agreed.
When Mr Miller comes, they are making a funny joke: they are pronouncing all the words wrongly. The teacher laughs. "If you go on with that, we're writing a dictation right now." That's a bad idea for a party! Oh look, Betty is coming. She's nicely dressed and holding a new record in her hands.
Tom is ill. He can't come today. But now he's phoning Peter. In the evening, they are all comfortably sitting in Peter's room and listening to Betty's fantastic record.

In the British Museum

One day Mr Hill took his class to the British Museum in London. They went there comfortably in a big bus. When they arrived at the museum and were moving through the gate they saw a hundred people waiting. "Oh, we're terribly late", said Mr Hill. After an hour they got inside. The rooms were larger than they supposed, and the things looked nicer and expensively priced. Some were safely kept behind glass.
In the afternoon the boys and girls hoped they could go down to Tower Bridge and see the river. Mr Hill agreed.
Truly, that was a finer day than a day at school!

2. Lernjahr

5. Wörter mit den Endungen **-o** *und* **-f**

Bei Wörtern, die auf ***-o*** oder ***-f*** enden, wird der Plural wie bei den anderen Substantiven durch das Anhängen von ***-s*** gebildet:

hipp**o**	-	hipp**os**	kangar**oo**	-	kangar**oos**
kil**o**	-	kil**os**	roo**f**	-	roo**fs**
radi**o**	-	radi**os**	chie**f**	-	chie**fs**

Manche Substantive, die auf ***-o*** enden, und die Verben **do** und **go** bilden den Plural beziehungsweise die dritte Person Singular auf ***-es:***

potat**o**	-	potato**es**
tomat**o**	-	tomato**es**
I d**o**	-	he do**es**
I g**o**	-	she go**es**

Präge dir die folgenden Substantive gut ein. Sie bilden den Plural auf ***-ves:***

kni**fe**	-	kni**ves**			
li**fe**	-	li**ves**	thie**f**	-	thie**ves**
wol**f**	-	wol**ves**	wi**fe**	-	wi**ves**

Aufgabe 14: Setze die Wörter, die in Klammern stehen, in den Plural.

1. In the (zoo) of many cities you can find (hippo) and (kangaroo).
2. Tourists often take (photo) of them.
3. An elephant weighs more (kilo) than a camel.
4. Be careful! (Thief) often carry (knife) with them!
5. The Indian (chief) knew how to grow (potato) and (tomato).
6. Their (wife) knew how to grow different kinds of (tobacco).
7. Later the settlers dried the tobacco on the (roof) of their houses.
8. (Wolf) have shorter (life) than horses.

Wenn du dir die Regeln gut eingeprägt hast, übe mit den folgenden zwei Diktaten:

At the zoo

Many big towns have zoos. On Sundays, husbands take their wives and children and go to see the animals. In the months of May and June it's very nice, because a lot of baby animals are there. The young wolves look like little dogs, and the baby hippos and kangaroos are really funny when they try to walk on their short legs. The people always take lots of photos. When the keeper* goes to the monkeys**, they all wait for him. Some sit on the roofs of their houses. He puts potatoes and tomatoes on a plate. They run for their lives to get their food.

* keeper = Wärter ** monkey = Affe

A safari in Africa

One of the most exciting holidays is a safari in Africa. By day the tourist doesn't do very much because it is very hot. But when the sun goes down behind the roofs of the hotels, men wait in their cars to drive the visitors out into the open country. They all take their cameras and knives from the shelves and hurry out. It is a fantastic moment when the big animals come to the water hole where the hippos are swimming. The biggest hippos are the chiefs of the group. If one of them leaves the water, all the others run away. Late at night the tourists come back for dinner. They have roast beef with tomatoes and potatoes. Then a boy goes round with a box. He sells little bags with different kinds of tobaccos of the country.

Wiederhole nochmal den „magischen Satz":

Happily sitting on their **potatoes** the **wolves** were **giving** their **parties**.

6. -s am Wortende

Du weißt, daß das *-s* am Ende von Substantiven die unterschiedlichste Bedeutung haben kann. Präge dir die folgenden Möglichkeiten gut ein und achte beim Diktat auf den Sinn der Wörter im Zusammenhang.

Der regelmäßige Plural wird durch das Anhängen von ***-s*** gebildet:

house - house**s**,
match - match**es**,
cap - cap**s**

Den Genitiv Singular eines Substantivs bildest du durch das Anhängen von **Apostroph + *s***:

Peter**'s** friend,
Judy**'s** pets,
a pupil**'s** school book

Substantive, die im Plural nicht auf -s enden, bilden den Genitiv durch das Anhängen von **Apostroph + *s***:

the children**'s** books,
an old people**'s** home,
the gentlemen**'s** toilets

Substantive, die im Plural auf ***-s*** enden, bilden den Genitiv durch das Anhängen eines **Apostrophs**:

the two boy**s'** bedroom,
the girl**s'** washroom,
the teenager**s'** club meeting

Im gesprochenen Englisch werden die Verben **is** und **has** oft zu ***-s*** verkürzt und mit einem **Apostroph** an das vorhergehende Pronomen angeschlossen:

He'**s** my friend. = He is my friend.
He'**s** got many pets. = He has got many pets.
It'**s** ten o'clock. = It is ten o'clock.

Aufgabe 15: Setze jeweils das *-s* in der richtigen Form an das Wortende.

A family in Dublin

1. The (O'Brian) live in Dublin.
2. Dublin is (Ireland) biggest city.
3. One of the Irish (people) hobbies is the greyhound races.
4. The (O'Brian) house is near the River Liffey.
5. Their (children) school is not far away.
6. They often read (book) about America.
7. Their two (boy) pen-friends live in Chicago.
8. (Patrick) pen-friend is 17 (year) old.
9. (Willy) friend works in a car factory.
10. (He) got a little pony.
11. His (parent) house is a bungalow.
12. Willy is happy about his (friend) invitation for the summer holiday.
13. (He) going to buy some presents before he flies.
14. He must remember that (Dublin) shops are closed on (Sunday).
15. In Ireland the (men) favourite place is the pub.
16. The (country) music is famous all over the world.

Hast du dir alle Regeln eingeprägt? Dann achte in den folgenden zwei Diktaten besonders auf das *-s* am Wortende:

A terrible school

Peter's school looks terrible. The boys' toilets are dirty, and there is no water in the girls' washroom. Look into the classroom: one boy's desk is broken, and other children's chairs are dirty with lemonade. Where's Mr Hill? He's in the teachers' room with Mrs Brown and Mr White. Judy's mouse is not in its cage. It's running around and looking into all the pupils' schoolbags. In the evening the children's fathers and mothers are coming. It's the parents' meeting. They are very angry. The next morning all the pupils clean their school.

After two hours everything looks fine. All the pupils' tables and chairs look clean. There are flowers on Mr Hill's desk, and a map with Britain's biggest towns is on the wall. The mouse is in its cage again. The calendar next to the door shows today's date.

Poor Tom

Peter's friend Tom is not at school. He's got a high temperature and must stay in bed. Tom's head is hot and red, and he doesn't want to read children's books. At night, his parents' bedroom door is open, so that Mrs Green can hear her poor boy's crying when he's feeling bad. Next morning Dr Robinson comes. He looks into the child's mouth and gives him some medicine. Then he says, "Sorry, Tom. You can't go out and play with your friends." In the afternoon, two girls from his class visit him. They bring a picture postcard with all the pupils' names on it. His English teacher's name is on a little present. But look, what's his dog bringing? In the animal's mouth is Tom's left shoe. The dog wants to play with him in the garden!

7. Unregelmäßige Verben

Die unregelmäßigen Verben im Englischen sind nicht schwer. Du mußt sie nur immer wieder üben. Du kannst sie dir leichter einprägen, wenn du dir eine eigene Liste anlegst und sie laufend ergänzt. Im übrigen wirst du die unregelmäßigen Verben im Englischen so oft brauchen, daß sie schnell „sitzen" werden. Präge dir die folgende Aufstellung, zum Teil nach Schreibgruppen geordnet, gut ein. Danach beherrschst du fast alle schwierigen unregelmäßigen Verben:

begin	beg**a**n	beg**u**n	anfangen
drink	drank	drunk	trinken
ring	rang	rung	läuten
sing	sang	sung	singen
swim	swam	swum	schwimmen
run	ran	run	laufen

Merke dir: Wenn im Infinitiv kein *a* vorkommt, steht in den anderen Formen *ou.*

bring	br**ou**ght	br**ou**ght	herbringen
buy	bought	bought	kaufen
think	thought	thought	denken, meinen

Merke dir: Wenn im Infinitiv ein *a* vorkommt, steht in den anderen Formen *au.*

catch	c**au**ght	c**au**ght	fangen

teach	taught	taught	lehren
blow	blew	blown	blasen, wehen
grow	grew	grown	wachsen
know	knew	known	kennen, wissen
throw	threw	thrown	werfen
feel	felt	felt	(sich) fühlen
keep	kept	kept	halten
leave	left	left	lassen, weggehen
send	sent	sent	schicken
sleep	slept	slept	schlafen
spell	spelt	spelt	buchstabieren
spend	spent	spent	verbringen/ (Geld) ausgeben
beat	beat	beaten	schlagen
become	became	become	werden
break	broke	broken	(zer)brechen
choose	chose	chosen	wählen
come	came	come	kommen
do	did	done	tun, machen
draw	drew	drawn	ziehen, zeichnen
drive	drove	driven	(Auto) fahren
eat	ate	eaten	(fr)essen

fall	fell	fallen	fallen
fly	flew	flown	fliegen
get	got	got	bekommen
give	gave	given	geben
go	went	gone	gehen, fahren
hide	hid	hidden	verstecken
lie	lay	lain	liegen
ride	rode	ridden	reiten, fahren
write	wrote	written	schreiben
see	saw	seen	sehen
show	showed	shown	zeigen
speak	spoke	spoken	sprechen
take	took	taken	nehmen
wear	wore	worn	(Kleidung) tragen
meet	met	met	treffen
feed	fed	fed	füttern
find	found	found	finden
hear	heard	heard	hören
lose	lost	lost	verlieren
make	made	made	machen
mean	meant	meant	bedeuten
read	read	read	lesen

pay	paid	paid	(be)zahlen
say	said	said	sagen
sell	sold	sold	verkaufen
tell	told	told	erzählen
shine	shone	shone	scheinen
sit	sat	sat	sitzen
stand	stood	stood	stehen
win	won	won	gewinnen

Aufgabe 16: Setze die folgende Geschichte ins Simple Past.

1. When we **go** to my aunt's in Brighton, Father first **drives** on the motorway, but then **makes** a turn to the south.
2. Mostly he **finds** a shorter route: this **means** we **get** to Aunt Margaret's village a bit earlier.
3. When we **come** round the corner, her dog Hercules **runs** to the car and almost **flies** into my arms.
4. We **leave** the car, **find** our way to the terrace, and Auntie **makes** tea and **brings** her famous apple pie.
5. In her house we always **feel** at home!
6. Uncle Bert **comes** a little later.
7. He **knows** so many things and **teaches** us fishing in a very special way:
8. He **blows** into his hands, **says** "Send me a fish" and **throws** the rod (= Angelrute) as far as possible.
9. If he **catches** an old shoe, he **is** not angry.
10. The fishing **makes** us so tired that we **sleep** for ten hours.

Aufgabe 17: Setze die Verben in Klammern ins Present Perfect oder Simple Past.

1. Mr McPherson is a taxi driver. He has just (drive) a Japanese tourist through London.
2. They have (see) the wonderful sights in Westminster and the City.

3. Three hours ago, Mr McPherson (meet) his guest at the Hilton Hotel, then he (show) him a map and they (choose) an interesting tour.
4. The Japanese has never (be) to Europe before. When they started he (sit) excitedly in the car and (begin) to ask hundreds of questions.
5. He even (draw) some sketches in a little book.
6. When he (pay) for the trip, he (give) his driver 100 pounds.
7. Mr McPherson (think) that his guest (feel) happy about his good service and (say) good-bye.
8. He (tell) him about some more interesting places.
9. Now, Mr McPherson has just (buy) a newspaper and has (read) a report about new cars.
10. Oh dear, now he finds out that he has (lose) the keys of the taxi.
11. Suddenly he remembers. He has (put) them on the counter (= Theke) in the newspaper shop and (leave) them there.

Übe die unregelmäßigen Verben mit den folgenden Testdiktaten:

The robber

Last night, when the Bensons were out, a robber broke into their house. He brought a sausage and fed their old dog. While the animal was eating it, he took a ladder and climbed up to a bedroom window. Nobody heard a sound when he threw a hammer against the glass. He saw very well where the things lay because the moon shone brightly. He found money and a cassette recorder. But when he left, he left his knife in the room. The Bensons gave it to the police, who found the right shopkeeper. He said to them, “Yes, I sold it to a man called ‘Big Mouth’. He didn’t pay for it!” Soon they caught him at a fast food restaurant in Brighton.

Don’t feed the animals!

Cathy and Sally went to the zoo. They took their little brother and rode there on their bikes. When they saw the animals they had a lot of fun. The budgies flew over their heads and caught a bit of Sally's sandwich. The wolves got up when they came and showed their teeth. Sally fed the ponies with sugar. Suddenly an angry man in uniform ran up to them and said, " Haven't you read the sign over there? Don't feed the animals!" Little Tom hid behind Cathy, because he thought the man spoke to him. After three hours the children began to get tired. So they left the zoo and rode home. They told their parents about the ponies. Mother thought that the man in the zoo meant that sugar is not good for ponies. She said, "I've seen horses with very bad and yellow teeth, because silly people gave them too many sweets."

In the mountains

In the Scottish highlands lots of tourists like to walk and to climb. Sometimes they think that this is not dangerous. Last Sunday a group of boys began to climb a mountain without good shoes. When the rain came, one of them lost his hold* and fell ten feet. Luckily a tree caught him and stopped his fall. The boy's friends thought it was a terrible accident. He spoke very slowly and said, "I think I've broken my arm." They pulled him up carefully and took him to the hospital at Loch Ness.

*hold = Halt

8. Gleichlautende Wörter und Formen (Homophone)

Sicher hast du schon gemerkt, daß es im Englischen Wörter gibt, die gleich klingen. Sie unterscheiden sich aber sowohl in ihrer Schreibweise als auch in ihrer Bedeutung voneinander. Welche Schreibweise die jeweils richtige ist, mußt du aus dem Satzzusammenhang erschließen. Wenn du die folgende Liste im Gedächtnis behältst, wirst du leichter auf diese Wörter aufmerksam:

been	-	bean	gewesen	-	Bohne
break	-	brake	brechen	-	Bremse
buy	-	Bye! - by	kaufen	-	Wiedersehen! - mit, vorbei, von
eye	-	I	Auge	-	ich
for	-	four	für	-	vier
here	-	hear	hier	-	hören
Hi!	-	high	Hallo!	-	hoch
hour	-	our	Stunde	-	unser
its	-	it's	sein	-	es ist
knew	-	new	wußte	-	neu
know	-	no	wissen	-	kein
(he) knows	-	nose	(er) kennt	-	Nase
(he) read	-	red	(er) las	-	rot
road	-	rode	Straße	-	fuhr
sail	-	sale	segeln	-	Verkauf

see -	sea	sehen -	Meer
son -	sun	Sohn -	Sonne
their - there -	they're	ihr(e) - dort -	sie sind
threw -	through	warf(en) -	durch
too - to -	two	auch - zu -	zwei
weak -	week	schwach -	Woche
wear -	where	(Kleid) tragen -	wo
won -	one	gewann -	ein
write -	right	schreiben -	richtig, rechts

Aufgabe 18: Setze für die Lautschrift die gleichlautenden, aber unterschiedlich geschriebenen Wörter an die jeweils richtige Stelle.

1. Have you ... shopping?
   Yes, but I forgot to buy ... soup. [bi:n]
   Oh no! I've waited ... hours ... my soup. [fɔ:]
2. Do you ... that there is ... salt in the box? [nəʊ]
3. If you stop the bike too quickly, the ... may ... . [breik]
4. Yesterday the holidays began; many people were on the ... to the south. They ... out to sea. [rəʊd]
5. In one ... we leave for France. It's ... first visit there. [aʊə]
6. Francis was the best in the competition; she ... the first prize: ... week in a hotel in Florida. [wʌn]
7. Alexandra was ... in our class. She only ... a few of us. [nju:]
8. Mark's father got an angry ... face when he ... his son's school report. [red]
9. Mary ... a new dress every day. ... the shop with such fantastic dresses? [weəz]
10. When you ... this exercise, please fill in the ... words. [rait]
11. And ... is your new disc jockey, Crazy Phil. Can you all ... me? [hiə]

12. ... was terribly afraid: the monster had one big ... in the middle of its face. [ai]
13. After the operation, Alison felt very ... . She had to stay in hospital for one ... . [wi:k]
14. Sandy, “It’s 1:58 by my watch.”
    Peggy, “Yes, my watch shows ... minutes ... ... , ..! [tu:]
15. The silly child ... a stone ... the window. [θru:]

Achte in den folgenden zwei Testdiktaten besonders auf die richtige Schreibweise der gleichlautenden Wörter:

Tom buys ice-cream

“Mum, I’m going to buy some ice-cream. I’m going by bike.” Tom rides down to the sea. There are lots of people playing in the sun. He can see young mothers with their little sons in the water. A girl with a red nose is running down the beach. Now Tom must hurry up. He knows that the shop closes at four o’clock. He looks for the right road and rides on. In the shop Mr Sweet says, “Hi Tom, I can see it in your eyes: you want some ice-cream.” The boy looks at Mr Sweet who is standing on a high ladder and answers, “Yes, I won one of the prizes in the school competition last week, it’s ten pounds. So please give me the biggest ice-cream that you have.”

Cats and dogs

Yesterday I thought I was dreaming. I saw that a red cat was running after a little dog. It was jumping down from a wall. This was new for me because I knew that dogs run after cats, and that they can do this for a long time. I took my bike and rode down our road. After half an hour I gave up and went home. Then I read in a book that there are cats that are not afraid of dogs. They can run very quickly and know that no dog can jump as high as they can. One year ago there was a race between a dog and a cat. The cat won.

9. Ähnlichlautende Wörter

Das Englische verwendet Laute, die in unserer Sprache nicht vorkommen und sich nur geringfügig voneinander unterscheiden, z.B. [ð] und [θ] für th, [s] und [z] für *s.* Durch diese geringen Lautveränderungen entstehen im Englischen völlig verschiedene Wörter. Es ist also wichtig, genau hinzuhören, um die Vokale und Konsonanten richtig zu erkennen.

Präge dir die folgenden Beispiele gut ein:

hat [hæt]	-	had [hæd]	Hut	-	hatte
head [hed]	-	hate [heit]	Kopf	-	hassen
hears [hiəz]	-	hers [hə:z]	hört	-	ihres
know [nəʊ]	-	now [naʊ]	wissen	-	jetzt
laugh [la:f]	-	love [lʌv]	lachen	-	lieben
listen [lisn]	-	lesson [lesn]	zuhören	-	Unterricht
May [mei]	-	my [mai]	Mai	-	mein
mouse [maʊs]	-	mouth [maʊθ]	Maus	-	Mund, Maul
pig [pig]	-	big [big]	Schwein	-	groß
plan [plæn]	-	plane [plein]	Plan	-	Flugzeug
quite [kwait]	-	quiet [kwaiət]	ganz,ziemlich	-	ruhig
ride [raid]	-	right [rait]	fahren,reiten	-	richtig
sick [sik]	-	thick [θik]	krank	-	dick
sing [siŋ]	-	thing [θiŋ]	singen	-	Sache

Aufgabe 19: In den folgenden Satzpaaren müssen sich die Wörter am Ende reimen. Wähle jeweils das richtige Wort aus.

1. The clown in the circus was very **fat**.
   He wore green trousers and a red ... . (had, hat)
2. Ladies and gentlemen, this is the end of the **show**!
   I'm the best entertainer, as you ... ! (no, know)
3. Benny came home rather **late**.
   Father said angrily, "That's what I ... !" (hate, head)
4. The children run out to **play**.
   It's spring now, now it's ... . (my, May)
5. We have got lots of animals in the **house**.
   Downstairs in the cellar there is a ... . (mouse, mouth)
6. Little Tommy is playing in the **rain**.
   He looks up and sees a ... . (plan, plane)
7. Disneyland near Paris is a great **sight**.
   I've been there, you're quite ...! (ride, right)

Aufgabe 20: Übersetze die in Klammern stehenden deutschen Begriffe und setze das Wort ein, das sich auf den fettgedruckten Ausdruck des vorhergehenden Satzes reimt.

1. Dover is a town in the **south**.
   Look, the hippo has a big ... . (Maus, Maul)
2. The zoo keeper **fed** the gorillas.
   One animal jumped on his ... . (Hut, Kopf)
3. **Dear** Mum and Dad, I'm writing from Munich.
   From my hotel I can ... the bells of the cathedral. (hier, hören, ihr)
4. Do you see the funny **cow** in the field?
   Yes, it's standing on two legs ... ! (kennen, jetzt)
5. Peter got a lot of presents; the best **thing** was a record player. He was so excited that he couldn't eat ... . (singen, irgend etwas)

Aufgabe 21: Errätst du die ähnlichklingenden Wortpaare? Setze sie an die richtige Stelle.

1. Brendan has eaten too much. His stomach is quite ... and he feels ... .
2. Please, boys and girls, ... to me; I'm starting a new ... .
3. If you want to tell me that your grandparents ... the Beatles, I must ... .
4. On a farm the most smelliest animal is the ... . It's funny that all people like to eat a ... cutlet from it!

Achte bei den folgenden Diktaten auf die richtige Schreibweise der ähnlichklingenden Wörter:

Poor bird !

It was the last Sunday in May. My mother was working in the garden. Because the sun was shining she had a green hat on her head. Suddenly our cat came quietly with a bird in its mouth. She put the bird gently on the steps. Mum was quite surprised and spoke to the animal, "Oh Kitty, what are you doing? You know you mustn't catch birds." Then she took the dead bird into her thick hands. It did not look very nice. She felt sick when she carried it away. At that moment, little Susy came out of the house. When she saw the bird in her mother's hand she was quite unhappy and said, "Poor little thing, now we can't see you fly and sing any more. I don't love that cat, that bad animal!"
Nobody in our family laughed.

The English lesson

Mr White is coming into the classroom for the English lesson. "Good morning everybody, please sit down and listen. You know that yesterday we read the unit about life on a farm. Look at your books.
On the picture on page thirty-seven you can see big pigs and a cat with a mouse in its mouth. The farmer's boy is riding a horse right onto the street. Some children are laughing and singing in the field. They love their life in the country. Their friends in the town often can't play so freely." Mr White has stopped because Peter is putting an old hat on his head." Peter, I hate this dirty hat, take it off and lis-ten to me, please!" The class is quiet now. They know quite well that their teacher is a litttle angry. But soon they all go on and talk about the picture again.

10. Schwierige Wörter

Einige englische Wörter haben eine ungewöhnliche Buchstabenkombination oder werden anders geschrieben als ausgesprochen. Diese Wörter solltest du dir gut einprägen. Wenn du die Wörter der folgenden Liste immer wieder übst, wirst du bald keine Rechtschreibfehler mehr machen:

a**u**nt	a:nt]	Tante
autu**mn**	[ɔ:təm]	Herbst
begg**a**r	[begə]	Bettler
bisc**ui**t	[biskit]	Keks
g**ui**tar	[gita:]	Gitarre
b**ui**lding	[bildiŋ]	Gebäude
b**u**sy	[bizi]	beschäftigt
g**ui**n**ea**-pig	[ginipig]	Meerschwein
budg**ie**	[bʌdʒi]	Wellensittich
calend**a**r	[kælendə]	Kalender
can**oe**	[kənu:]	Kanu
sh**oe**	[ʃu:]	Schuh
car**r**ot	[kærət]	Karotte
par**r**ot	[pærət]	Papagei
catalog**ue**	[kætəlɔg]	Katalog
dialog**ue**	[daiəlɔg]	Dialog
clim**b**	[klaim]	klettern

thum**b**	[θʌm]	Daumen
c**o**c**oa**	[kəʊkəʊ]	Kakao
caf**é**	[kæfei]	Café
co**ffee**	[kɔfi]	Kaffee
c**o**l**ou**r	[kʌlə]	Farbe
d**au**ghter	[dɔ:tə]	Tochter
depart**ure**	[dipa:tʃə]	Abfahrt, -flug
enough	[inʌf]	genug
g**u**ess	[ges]	raten
g**u**est	[gest]	Gast
g**ui**de	[gaid]	Führer
head**ache**	[hedeik]	Kopfschmerzen
i**s**land	[ailənd]	Insel
j**ui**ce	[dʒu:s]	Saft
j**ou**rney	[dʒə:ni]	Reise
knee	[ni:]	Knie
knock	[nɔk]	klopfen
ma**ch**ine	[məʃi:n]	Maschine
nei**gh**bour	[neibə]	Nachbar
programm**e**	[prəʊgrəm]	Programm
sail**o**r	[seilə]	Seemann
visit**o**r	[vizitə]	Besucher

sheri**ff**	[ʃerif]	Sheriff
st**o**mach	[stʌmək]	Magen
th**ou**s**a**nd	[θaʊzənd]	tausend
thr**ough**	[θru:]	durch
w**o**m**e**n	[wimin]	Frauen
M**o**nday	[mʌndi]	Montag
T**ue**sday	[tju:zdi]	Dienstag
We**d**nesday	[wenzdi]	Mittwoch
Th**u**rsday	[θə:zdi]	Donnerstag
Fr**i**day	[fraidi]	Freitag
Sat**ur**day	[sætədi]	Sonnabend, Samstag
S**u**nday	[sʌndi]	Sonntag

Hast du dir die Wörter gut eingeprägt, dann überprüfe dein Wissen anhand der folgenden Diktate:

In the pet shop

Aunt Betty has got a pet shop. She sells birds, all kinds of animals and things for them. Guess what's in the cage over there. It's a budgie and a parrot. Their colours are green and yellow. The guinea-pigs are eating carrots. You can also buy biscuits for dogs or guides on keeping pets. On Wednesday the shop is closed. So many visitors come on Tuesday and Thursday: women with their little daughters, schoolboys, and old people. Our neighbour has got a big cat, so she also buys things here.

Shopping with the Browns

The Browns always go shopping on Saturday morning. Mrs Brown needs things for the weekend. Today she is buying coffee, cocoa, carrots, eggs, and milk, because she has guests on Sunday. Mary goes to the pet shop and gets biscuits for Fluffy, their dog. She likes to look at the parrot with its nice colours. She tries to have a dialogue with him, but he only wants a biscuit and takes it from her thumb. Peter is in the music shop. He loves guitars and wants to see the programmes of the next pop concert. After an hour they all meet in the café. Mum has a cup of coffee, the children drink orange juice. Suddenly Mary cries out, “Oh Peter, look, there is juice on your knees! You haven’t been careful enough!” His pair of jeans is wet and dirty now and is the colour of guinea pigs.

Mr Brown’s Saturday morning

On Saturdays when his family is shopping, Mr Brown is busy at home. Now in autumn he works in the garden. He takes the ladder and climbs the apple-tree to pick the last fruits. After that he must clean the canoe, because on their last journey to a little island it got dirty. Then he talks with his neighbour about a catalogue of fruit trees. Suddenly somebody is knocking at the door. It’s a beggar. Mr Brown gives him one pound. Then he goes through the house and looks for his calendar. When he finds out that guests are coming tomorrow, he says, “Oh, I must hurry up. There are no drinks in the house, and it’s my job to buy them. Where are my shoes?” He calls his dog, “Fluffy, you silly dog, you have got my brown shoes! Where are they? You’re giving me a headache!” Fluffy runs and comes back with one shoe in his mouth. The other shoe is lying behind the washing machine.

Übung macht den Meister! Du hast gewiß schon gemerkt, daß du viel sicherer an eine Klassenarbeit herangehst, wenn du nicht erst im letzten Augenblick den ganzen Stoff auf einmal durcharbeitest. Gewöhne dir ein regelmäßiges Wiederholen des Wortschatzes an, dann verlierst du nicht den Überblick und kannst dir deine Arbeitszeit besser einteilen. Nimm dir alle paar Tage ein Diktat vor, du kannst zwischen kürzeren und längeren auswählen. Du wirst bald merken, daß du den Schwierigkeitsgrad schnell steigern kannst und die nächste Stufe leicht schaffst. Am besten ist es, wenn dir jemand die Texte in der üblichen Weise vorliest: jeden Sinnabschnitt zweimal mit Satzzeichen, dann abschließend das ganze Diktat nochmals ohne Satzzeichen. Du kannst dir aber auch die Texte auf Cassette sprechen lassen und damit selbständig arbeiten. Achte beim Üben von Anfang an darauf, daß die gleiche Schreib- und Diktiergeschwindigkeit eingehalten wird, wie im Unterricht gefordert.
Wie Satzzeichen auf Englisch diktiert werden, erfährst du auf Seite 7.

Zu deiner eigenen Kontrolle solltest du deine Diktate sorgfältig auswerten. Stelle fest, welche Fehler du sehr häufig machst. Sind es Schreibfehler, besonders bei schwierigeren Vokabeln, wiederhole am besten schriftlich den durchgenommenen Wortschatz. Du kannst dir auch eine Wortkartei anlegen, in der du die Worte sammelst, die du immer wieder falsch schreibst, und sie gezielt üben. Hast du gegen die Regeln der Grammatik verstoßen, schlage die entsprechenden Kapitel im ersten Teil dieses Buches nach.

Noch eine Bemerkung zu unbekannten Wörtern in den folgenden Diktaten: Da die Texte sich weitgehend an den Themen deiner Schulbücher orientieren, diese aber in ihrer Gestaltung sehr unterschiedlich sind, kann es gerade am Anfang vorkommen, daß du das eine oder andere Wort noch nicht gelernt hast und es falsch schreibst. In diesem Fall zählst du den Fehler natürlich nicht mit. Suche dir zuerst immer die Diktate aus, deren Inhalte im Unterricht schon vorgekommen oder vom Thema her ähnlich sind.

Good morning

Here's Mr King. He's a teacher.

Hello, boys and girls.

Good morning, Mr King.

What's your name?

I'm Tom. I'm from Britain.

Look at that boy. He's in my class.

He's from Germany. His name is Peter.

How old are you, Peter?

I'm eleven. It's nice in the class.

59 words

Diktatauswertung:

Welche Wörter habe ich falsch geschrieben?

____

____

____

____

Gesamtfehlerzahl:________

The American teacher

Who's that ? It's not Mr Green, our German teacher.

Good morning, boys and girls. I'm your new English teacher. I'm American. I'm from New York. Nice to meet you. Where are you from?

The boys and girls in this class are from London, but Gisela is from Germany.

Well, take your books. They are very nice and not very old.

68 words

Diktatauswertung:

Welche Wörter habe ich falsch geschrieben?

Gesamtfehlerzahl:_______

School things

Hello Tim. You've got a big school bag. What's in it?

How many books have you got?

Look, here's my English book and there's my German book. I've got a nice green pencil-case with a lot of pens and pencils, a rubber and a ruler. Where's my exercise-book? It's not here. Have you got one for me? I've got a banana for you.

Thank you very much, that's nice.

81 words

Diktatauswertung:

Welche Wörter habe ich falsch geschrieben?

____

____

____

Gesamtfehlerzahl:________

A new family

Hello, I'm Peter. There's a new car over there. It's from Germany. And here's David and his family. David is the new boy in my class. Hello David. Is this your mother?

Yes Peter, and here are my father and my sister Barbara. She's eleven. We've got a dog, too. He's under the car. His name is Monster, but he's small. He's our best friend.

77 words

Diktatauswertung:

Welche Wörter habe ich falsch geschrieben?

Gesamtfehlerzahl:________

A new girl

Betty is a new girl in my class. She's ten. Oh, here's my teacher, Mr Hill.

Good morning, sit down, please.

Mr Hill, here's Betty. She's new here. Her sister isn't at school. She's five.

Hello, Betty, where are you from?

I'm from London. Look, here's my English book. It's new.

Very good, Betty. Oh, look at that boy. He's late. Sorry, Mr Hill.

Where is your book?

Oh, it's not here. It's not in my school bag.

93 words

Diktatauswertung:

Welche Wörter habe ich falsch geschrieben?

Gesamtfehlerzahl: ________

Our home

My parents have got a nice little house with a garden. The car is in the garage. Our house has got three rooms downstairs: a living-room, a dining-room, and the kitchen. Upstairs there's Kevin's room behind Mum and Dad's bedroom. My room has got a big window and a balcony. The toilet is in the bathroom. The house isn't very old, but in the garden there's a big apple-tree.

74 words

Diktatauswertung:

Welche Wörter habe ich falsch geschrieben?

Gesamtfehlerzahl: ______

Mary's room

My sister's room is upstairs and has got a small balcony. Mary's bed is near the window. In her cupboard she has got lots of things. The record-player is on the table. Oh look, there are some cassettes on her chair. One is by a pop star and his music band. And where is her cat, Garfield? Oh dear, he's sitting on the shelf* and looking down.

"Garfield, come down!"

The cat is coming, and with him ten books are falling to the floor.

*shelf = Regal

87 words

Diktatauswertung:

Welche Wörter habe ich falsch geschrieben?

Gesamtfehlerzahl: ________

Having tea with the Browns

Peter, a boy from Germany, is visiting his new friend Mike in the afternoon. The Browns are sitting in their dining-room. There are four cups and saucers on the table, a tea pot, sugar, milk, and a plate with fine biscuits.

“Come in, Peter, and have a cup of tea with us. This is how we do it in Britain.”

“Oh thank you, Mrs Brown, that’s very nice. At home I only drink hot milk or chocolate.”

“Sit down on this chair, Peter. How old are you?”

“I’m thirteen, and my sister is nine. She’s at the school in London Road.”

“Oh, where is Mike? He’s upstairs. Go up to him, he’s playing a music cassette.”

“Thank you, for the tea and the biscuits, Mrs Brown.”

126 words

Diktatauswertung:

Welche Wörter habe ich falsch geschrieben?

____

____

____

____

____

Gesamtfehlerzahl: ________

In the pet shop

Sally is standing in Mrs Winter's animal shop.

"Hello Sally, are you looking for something? How is your hamster?"

"Thank you, Mrs Winter, it's fine, but now it's sleeping till the evening. Have you got some new pets here?"

"Oh yes, Sally, look at the big cage over there. Can you see the young dogs with long ears and brown eyes? Their mother is ten years old, but her two babies are all right."

"And what's over there in the water?"

"Well, we've got fifteen new goldfish. You can watch them, but please don't take them out!"

"I must go home now, my hamster's waiting for me and its food. Good-bye Mrs Winter."

113 words

Diktatauswertung:

Welche Wörter habe ich falsch geschrieben?

Gesamtfehlerzahl: ________

Clothes

Children in Britain must wear school uniforms. Look at Kate. She's got a blue skirt and a grey pullover for winter, or a white blouse for summer. Her brother John is in class 2 B. He has got blue trousers and a grey blazer. The boys and girls can't wear jeans at school. You can see by their uniforms where they go to school. Must they wear the same socks and shoes, too? Of course not. They can wear brown or black shoes, or green and yellow socks.
In Germany the children all wear the same clothes, too. They all have got jeans!

106 words

Diktatauswertung:

Welche Wörter habe ich falsch geschrieben?

____

____

____

____

____

Gesamtfehlerzahl:________

A bike ride

"Hello Bob, what are you doing now? Are you learning German?"

"No, there's no homework today. Mr Hill is ill. Let's go for a ride. Wait a moment, I must get my pump from our garage, because my tyre* is flat. Are you ready?"

"OK Bob. Where can we ride? My aunt has got a shop down by the sea. We can make a stop there. Perhaps we can get some biscuits."

"That's good, Peter. I like biscuits."

Now the boys are on the road. Oh dear, Bob's tyre is flat again. He must go to a repair shop. There's a man over there.

"Hello, can you help us? Where's a repair shop for bikes?"

The man is very nice. He takes the bike to his house. Now he's repairing the tyre.

*tyre [taiə] = Reifen

142 words

Diktatauswertung:

Welche Wörter habe ich falsch geschrieben?

Gesamtfehlerzahl: ________

Hobbies

Colin is writing about hobbies for the school magazine. He is asking his friends in the classroom.

"David, what's your hobby?"

"Well, I like playing football with other boys. Swimming is also very nice in summer. Then I can go to the swimming-pool."

"OK, now what about Sally?"

"Well, look here. I'm painting a picture of our garden. Of course I can't do it during the lesson, but Mr Brown isn't coming."

"Thank you, Sally, and now you, Bob. What's that on your table?"

"Oh, this is a letter to my pen-friend* in Berlin. I'm writing to him, and it's nice to get an answer later. This afternoon I'm playing in a band. That's very funny, because my dog is singing to the music."

"Very good, Bob. And who's there? Sarah, have you got a hobby, too?"

"I haven't got much time. I must watch TV and listen to cassettes!"

Poor Sarah!

*pen-friend = Brieffreund(in)

162 words

Diktatauswertung:

Welche Wörter habe ich falsch geschrieben?

____

____

____

____

____

Gesamtfehlerzahl:_______

Peggy's day

It's a quarter past seven. Peggy is in bed. Mother comes into her room.

"Good morning, get up please. It's time for breakfast."

Two minutes later the girl is in the bathroom. At half past seven she is sitting at the table. There's hot milk in the cup and a sandwich on the plate.

Now it's nine o'clock. School starts with an English lesson. At a quarter to one they have lunch at school. In the afternoon there is a football match till three o'clock.

Now it's ten to five. Peggy is playing with her two dogs in the garden.

At half past seven Dad comes home. The family is sitting in the dining-room. The dogs can't come in because there are sausages* on the table. Later Peggy hasn't got time to watch TV. She has got a nice book up in her bedroom.

*sausage [sɔsidʒ] = Würstchen

152 words

Diktatauswertung:

Welche Wörter habe ich falsch geschrieben?

Gesamtfehlerzahl:________

Down by the sea

It's a warm Sunday in August. The Browns are having breakfast. They are talking about what they can do. Peter has got a good plan: "Let's go swimming in the sea." At eleven o'clock they are all down there with lots of other people. Mum has got a big basket for lunch. Of course her family is hungry. Dad is putting away the paper. "Well, let's have a nice picnic here on the sand. Mum can go swimming, and we can put the things on the plates. There's coke, we've got lots of sandwiches, apples, and a cake."

Later they play ball. Peter and Sarah win the match. In the evening there are lots of cars on the road, so it's nine o'clock when the family gets back to the house.

141 words

Diktatauswertung:

Welche Wörter habe ich falsch geschrieben?

Gesamtfehlerzahl:_______

A letter from Scotland

Dear Alexander,

Thank you for your letter and the photos of your family. Your parents must be nice, and you have got a lot of pets. Your brother is a funny boy! Why has he got a rat on his arm? I think rats are horrible.

Is school over at one o'clock in Germany? That's very good, because in the afternoon you can play with your friends. Or have you got a lot of homework? Here in Scotland we can't go home till half past three.

Are you coming in August? We can do lots of nice things. Have you got a bike? When you are here, you can have my mother's bike.

Please write soon. I'm waiting!

Love from

Donald

127 words

Diktatauswertung:

Welche Wörter habe ich falsch geschrieben?

Gesamtfehlerzahl: ________

The old castle

Susan lives in a village. If she rides her bike for half an hour, she comes to an old castle. Today she is there with Sandy, her school friend. She wants to show her friend a nice room where nobody can find her. They climb down the old steps. Suddenly Sandy calls, “Help, help, I can’t see you any more.” Susan goes back, but can’t find the right way. She is crying now and looking for the steps that lead her out. After ten terrible minutes she sees an open door. She runs outside, and there’s Sandy. The two girls are very happy.

107 words

Diktatauswertung:

Welche Wörter habe ich falsch geschrieben?

Gesamtfehlerzahl:_______

How to give a party

Are you giving a party? Here are some tips:

Start shopping for the party early. It's not much fun when your friends are coming and you haven't got the drinks and food at home. First you must buy coloured paper for the party room. You can put it round the lamps. At the shop on the corner or in the supermarket you get coke, lemonade, or juice. What about making your own cake? It's much more fun eating a cake than biscuits. Have you got any music cassettes? Be careful. If the pop music is too loud, the people can't talk and tell stories. Singing is also a fine thing, because all the boys and girls can do it together. Good luck!

130 words

Diktatauswertung:

Welche Wörter habe ich falsch geschrieben?

Gesamtfehlerzahl: ______

Going to a party

Have you got an invitation to a birthday party? Oh, that's great!

First, of course, you must tell your friend that you can come. Perhaps you can write a postcard or a letter. You can say that you are very happy about the invitation. Now think of the present. What are your friend's hobbies? Does she like books or games, or has she got a pet? Don't give her your old toys or chocolates from last Easter! It's very nice to have good ideas about what you can play at the party. It's not much fun to just sit around and eat. What about karaoke*? All the boys and girls laugh when you try to sing like Elvis Presley!

*karaoke [kæraəʊki] = Imitationssingen

126 words

Diktatauswertung:

Welche Wörter habe ich falsch geschrieben?

____

____

____

____

____

Gesamtfehlerzahl:________

People in our street

Mr and Mrs Brown are our neighbours*. They are eighty and seventy-six years old, but still live in their own home. Mr Brown often takes his dog and goes shopping because his wife can't walk so well. She has got bad legs. So she stays at home. Sometimes she makes her famous cake with apples and chocolate pieces. Then she invites us for tea. Mr Brown likes tea, too. He tells us fantastic stories about the old days. You know, he is a taxi driver, but can't work anymore, of course.

In winter, when it is cold and wet, we help the Browns with the shopping. Peter likes this job very much, because Mrs Brown always gives him a little money for it.

*neighbours [neibəz] = Nachbarn

127 words

Diktatauswertung:

Welche Wörter habe ich falsch geschrieben?

____

____

____

____

____

Gesamtfehlerzahl:_______

Our friends from India

There is a new girl in our class. Her parents come from India. Her name is Sari. She is a nice girl with black hair, a brown face and friendly eyes. Her English is not very good, but she learns quickly. Sari finds life in England very interesting. She tells us that the Indian people are very poor.

Today she is in our garden. She is telling us about elephants. She can ride on them. If people in India have to move to a new home, they pack their things onto an elephant. Sari's father works at the post office. Her mother gives lessons in the evening. She teaches Indian dancing.

It's nice that they are living in our town.

125 words

Diktatauswertung:

Welche Wörter habe ich falsch geschrieben?

Gesamtfehlerzahl: ________

Painting a room

The house in London Street has four flats. Tina and her brother Dave live with their mother and three hamsters in one of them. Tina is fifteen now, but the wallpaper* is still the same as when she was a baby. You can see Mickey Mouse and Uncle Donald on it. Its colour is pink and yellow. Dave's friends always laugh when they come and look into the room. So she wants to take it down and paint the wall white. On Saturday her cousin Betty is helping her. They must put the table, the bed and the cupboard into Dave's room. They work for two days. On Sunday evening they can put up the picture of Tina's favourite pop star. Of course they are terribly tired, but very happy, too.

*wallpaper = Tapete

134 words

Diktatauswertung:

Welche Wörter habe ich falsch geschrieben?

Gesamtfehlerzahl: ________

Through the year

January and February are cold months. When we can't go outside, we like to sit in a comfortable chair and read stories. In the long evenings we can also watch an interesting film. The cat is inside, too. There are no mice in the garden. March and April bring spring to the country. But if there is a lot of rain and wind, we can catch a bad cold. On Mother's Day in May the families often go by bike to nice villages or picnic grounds. In June and July the end of the school year comes nearer, and the children must work hard. But then, in August and September, they go on holiday. In autumn many people go to farms and pick apples or potatoes. Then, at the end of the year, we all wait for the great day: Christmas.

145 words

Diktatauswertung:

Welche Wörter habe ich falsch geschrieben?

____

____

____

____

____

Gesamtfehlerzahl: _______

The lost ticket

Tom's cousin Betty from Scotland is staying with Tom's family for the Easter holidays. They live in Windsor, but today the two children are in London. They want to see the football match between England and France. After a visit to the British Museum they take the underground to the stadium. Suddenly a ticket inspector comes onto the train. "Can I see your ticket, please?" he asks Betty. "Just a moment, please," says Betty and looks for it in her bag. "Oh dear, I can't find it, I have lost it somewhere." The inspector laughs, "I've heard this story very often. Sorry, you've got to pay 20 pounds." Suddenly Tom says, "Wait, I've got the ticket. I put our two tickets in my pocket when I bought them."

134 words

Diktatauswertung:

Welche Wörter habe ich falsch geschrieben?

____

____

____

____

____

Gesamtfehlerzahl: ________

In London

On their way to Germany the Millers stay in London. Their hotel is near Green Park, so they can get to many interesting places by underground. At eleven o'clock they are standing at Buckingham Palace with lots of other tourists. The Queen is in the Palace, so a flag* is at the top of the building. Half an hour later they can see the beautiful show: the Queen's guard** riding on horses, the band playing music, and all the colours of the uniforms. One of the guards has a big dog with him!

In the afternoon the Millers walk through Westminster. Big Ben looks nice with its new clock shining in the sun. Down by the river there is a kiosk where they buy some ice-cream. It's late, so they go back to the hotel.

* flag = Fahne ** guard [ga:d] = Wache

138 words

Diktatauswertung:

Welche Wörter habe ich falsch geschrieben?

Gesamtfehlerzahl:________

Beautiful Britain

Many Germans think of London when they hear about Britain. Of course it's a great city and you can visit fantastic places there. But Britain is a big country like Germany, with lots of nice towns, castles, mountains and rivers.

West of London you can find holiday places for old people, families and children. Everything there is great fun: swimming, riding, playing tennis, visiting old churches and eating in restaurants. Stay in a hotel, or have bed and breakfast at a farm, or go to a camping site!

Scotland is nice, too. Near Loch Ness*, there is a museum where you can see photos of Nessie*! Perhaps you can get a horse and ride over the quiet mountains and through the little villages, and you may find new friends there, too.

* Evtl. buchstabieren

135 words

Diktatauswertung:

Welche Wörter habe ich falsch geschrieben?

____

____

____

Gegen welche Rechtschreibregel verstoße ich am häufigsten?

____

Gesamtfehlerzahl:________

Flying to America

Aunt Barbara and Uncle Bill live in New York. Last week a letter came with an invitation for this summer. It was an exciting time for Carol and her family to plan the trip.

Today their flight leaves at nine o'clock. At the airport they have to find their way to the right plane. There are crowds of passengers with them. At last they are on the plane, and soon they can look down at the clouds. The flight takes about seven hours. When they arrive in New York, Carol is quite surprised when she looks at the big clock in the restaurant: it's just eleven o'clock. Now she remembers what her teacher told them about America. They are five hours behind Britain. Suddenly she feels a hand on her shoulder. She turns round and looks into Uncle Bill's face. He is laughing and happy to see the girl again after five years.

158 words

Diktatauswertung:

Welche Wörter habe ich falsch geschrieben?

____

____

____

____

____

Gegen welche Rechtschreibregel verstoße ich am häufigsten?

____

Gesamtfehlerzahl:________

Friends in America

After seven hours on the plane Carol arrives in New York. While she is still in the air, she can see Manhattan. It is exciting to see the blue water of the sea and the windows of the skyscrapers shining in the sun. After the landing, Uncle Bill drives her home. He and Aunt Barbara live out of town. There is no fence around their house. In the big garden Carol can see a grill for barbecues. Aunt Barbara is showing her a cage with rabbits and a fantastic swimming-pool. Carol is happy and says, "I'm going to have a great time with you." In the evening she is very tired. Uncle Bill knows why: in Britain it's two o'clock in the morning now, and the poor girl has been awake for eighteen hours!

139 words

Diktatauswertung:

Welche Wörter habe ich falsch geschrieben?

____

____

____

____

____

Gegen welche Rechtschreibregel verstoße ich am häufigsten?

____

Gesamtfehlerzahl: ________

Holiday on a farm

One evening, John and Mary asked their parents about the summer holidays, “After our visit to France last year, why can’t we stay in England? How about two weeks on a farm?” Their parents thought for a moment and found it a good idea. In July they drove to a small village near Hatfield. There were about twenty farms around a beautiful old church. They saw cows and horses in the fields, and lots of ducks were swimming on a river.

Their farm was near the wood. Mother liked the flowers in the front garden. The farmer and his wife said welcome to them. They soon felt at home. Father helped in the fields, John tried to ride on a pig and Mary learned how to milk a cow. The days went by very quickly. On their way home they all agreed to come back next year.

151 words

Diktatauswertung:

Welche Wörter habe ich falsch geschrieben?

____

____

____

____

Gegen welche Rechtschreibregel verstoße ich am häufigsten?

____

Gesamtfehlerzahl: ________

A farmer's day

Many people think that life in the country is comfortable and beautiful. You are always out in the fresh air, and nobody is in a hurry. That's true, but the farmer and his family have got a lot to do.

Every day at five o'clock they have to milk the cows, even on Sundays. After breakfast they have to clean the cowshed and the smelly pig sty*. Work in the field is hard and often takes a long time because you need fine and dry weather for it.

The farmer's wife is very busy, too. She feeds the animals, keeps the house and garden tidy, collects the chickens' eggs, and makes lunch.

In winter there is a lot of repair work. Some machines are broken, and the wind blows through open parts in the shed.

You see, life on a farm never gets boring!

* pig sty = Schweinestall

148 words

Diktatauswertung:

Welche Wörter habe ich falsch geschrieben?

____

____

____

Gegen welche Rechtschreibregel verstoße ich am häufigsten?

____

Gesamtfehlerzahl:________

Castle ghosts

Britain is famous for its old castles. Of course, people know a lot of stories about them. They often believe that the ghosts of dead kings are still living there. When tourists visit the castles, they like to climb up dark stairs and listen for strange sounds. They look for shadows behind doors and open parts in the walls. When a bird flies over their heads, they feel afraid. It's the biggest adventure to walk around a castle in a thunderstorm. In the short, bright light things look terrible, and the thunder is like the sound of a monster.

Boys often laugh and find it funny when girls are afraid of ghosts. But at night they dream of these terrible pictures, too. Then they wake up and call for help.

133 words

Diktatauswertung:

Welche Wörter habe ich falsch geschrieben?

____

____

____

____

____

Gegen welche Rechtschreibregel verstoße ich am häufigsten?

____

Gesamtfehlerzahl:________

Robin Hood

All British children know the story of Robin Hood. He lived about 800 years ago and helped the poor people fight against the Sheriff of Nottingham*. Why did he do that?

The king and his rich men took everything from the farmers and had a comfortable life in their castles. But the people in the villages often had nothing to eat, and their children were sick and sometimes died. It was the Sheriff's job to take away their cows and horses. Many of them had to leave their homes.

Robin Hood took a few men and robbed the rich people when they rode to the market in the town. Then he gave the money to the hungry families. Of course the Sheriff tried to catch these men, but they were too clever.

* Evtl. buchstabieren

134 words

Diktatauswertung:

Welche Wörter habe ich falsch geschrieben?

____

____

____

____

Gegen welche Rechtschreibregel verstoße ich am häufigsten?

____

Gesamtfehlerzahl:_______

At the seaside

Every year Oliver waits for the summer holidays, when he can stay with his uncle on the south coast. Uncle Kevin is a fisherman and over sixty years old. But he still has his boat and takes the boy out onto the sea.

Last August they were fishing again, and the seagulls were following them with their cries. In the afternoon a storm came up, and the boat moved from one side to the other. Suddenly it turned over and the two people fell into the water. Oliver was a good swimmer, but where was his uncle? The boy called for help and swam to the beach. The police came and they all drove along the coast. After one mile they saw a man in wet clothes, holding up his hand: Uncle Kevin. Later he told them his story, "I tried to hold on to the boat, and the wind drove me to this place."

158 words

Diktatauswertung:

Welche Wörter habe ich falsch geschrieben?

____

____

____

____

____

Gegen welche Rechtschreibregel verstoße ich am häufigsten?

____

Gesamtfehlerzahl: ________

A visit to the hospital

Tom was not very lucky last week. He fell off his bike because he didn't see a stone on the road. He broke his left leg and now has to stay in hospital.

The room where he is lying is bright and clean. The nurses and his doctor are friendly. But it's boring to lie in bed, and he can't always watch TV. But in the afternoon there is a great surprise. His school friends are coming. Of course they have brought some presents. Peggy puts a puzzle on his bed, Peter has collected some photos of football stars for him, and Kevin has found his old cassette recorder. His father repaired it, so they can play music on it now.

Suddenly a nurse opens the door and says, "Please don't play the music so loudly. The old man next door is very ill and must sleep." So they start to do the puzzle.

158 words

Diktatauswertung:

Welche Wörter habe ich falsch geschrieben?

Gegen welche Rechtschreibregel verstoße ich am häufigsten?

Gesamtfehlerzahl:

A bike race

On the last school day, class 3 B had a bike race against 3 D. Three boys and two girls had good bikes and checked them for the day. Tommy's brakes were broken, Sandra's tyre was flat, and her brother's saddle was too high for her. But they repaired everything, and on the day before the race they met to practise on the track.*

Then on Wednesday the exciting moment came. Ten riders were waiting at the start. The sports teacher gave a sign and the race started. First Sandra overtook two boys, but before the second hill she touched another girl's wheel and nearly fell. After the hill, Tommy and a boy from the other class were neck to neck, but then they had to cross the mud. Tommy wanted to jump over it, but came down too early. He had to push his bike out of the track with a dirty face. Poor boy!

* track = hier: Rennstrecke

159 words

Diktatauswertung:

Welche Wörter habe ich falsch geschrieben?

Gegen welche Rechtschreibregel verstoße ich am häufigsten?

Gesamtfehlerzahl: ________

Charly's friend

Jenny's favourite hobby is riding horses. Today she is practising for a competition on Saturday. People from all over England take part in* the race, and the girl wants to be among the best.

The track is outside the town, and she has to teach Charly, her horse, to jump over three fences. But the animal always stops before the third one and turns his head. Jenny is very angry, but she knows that she mustn't shout. She starts again and again and makes the horse run fast. What can she do? Suddenly there is another horse on the other side of the field. Charly sees the horse, jumps easily over the three fences and runs up to his friend.

Who is cheering over there on the road? Jenny's friend Betty laughs and says, "You're the best rider in Britain!"

* to take part in = teilnehmen an

143 words

Diktatauswertung:

Welche Wörter habe ich falsch geschrieben?

Gegen welche Rechtschreibregel verstoße ich am häufigsten?

Gesamtfehlerzahl:

Robert is ill

It's a bad day for Robert. Tomorrow his class has an important German test. The boy is sitting in front of his book and doesn't understand the grammar. In the last few weeks he didn't have much time for school because his team played in many football matches.

In the evening, he suddenly gets a funny feeling in his stomach and his head aches. His mother looks into his mouth and says, "Oh dear, your throat is as red as fire." She checks his temperature. It's almost 39 degrees. Robert feels so bad that he wants to go to bed.

In the night he dreams of monsters with German words on their backs. Of course he can't write the test next morning. Dr Black comes at eleven o'clock and asks Robert's mother to fetch some medicine. He is surprised that the boy is not at all unhappy about his illness.

Are you surprised, too?

159 words

Diktatauswertung:

Welche Wörter habe ich falsch geschrieben?

____

____

____

____

____

Gegen welche Rechtschreibregel verstoße ich am häufigsten?

____

Gesamtfehlerzahl: ________

Everybody likes sports

Most people are interested in sports programmes on TV. When there is a football match between Italy and Scotland, or an international tennis competition in Australia, the roads are empty. But many people think it's more fun to play sports in a club or a team. Boys often love football, basketball or table tennis more than other things. Tennis, swimming, and riding are girls' favourite sports. If you want to be successful, you must practise a lot and take part in the training. Sometimes children think they are not fit enough for any sport. They are wrong, because you needn't be number one to have fun. The best players are not always the best team partners. Sometimes young people are handicapped* and cannot walk anymore. But they take part in races and play ball in their wheel-chairs**. That's a great thing!

* to be handicapped = behindert sein
** wheel-chair = Rollstuhl

146 words

Diktatauswertung:

Welche Wörter habe ich falsch geschrieben?

Gegen welche Rechtschreibregel verstoße ich am häufigsten?

Gesamtfehlerzahl:________

Daddy is in hospital

Mr Carter didn't feel well for about a month. At last his wife told him to see their doctor for a check-up. On Tuesday he went there. Dr Miller asked him about his problems. When he heard that Mr Carter was always tired, didn't want to eat much and had a terrible stomach ache, he said, "You must go to hospital. They've got to find out what's wrong with you."

When their Dad was lying in hospital, John and Betty saw that there were some jobs to do. "Who's going to walk the dog? What about the high grass in the garden? The car is terribly dirty." When Mrs Carter came home from her visit to her husband, she found her children in the living-room. The TV was on, the dog was sleeping, the boy was reading the newspaper, and Betty had Dad's pipe* in her mouth. When Mum asked what they were doing, they only said, "We have Dad's job now. Look at the garden and the garage!"

* pipe = Pfeife

175 words

Diktatauswertung:

Welche Wörter habe ich falsch geschrieben?

Gegen welche Rechtschreibregel verstoße ich am häufigsten?

Gesamtfehlerzahl:________

The sick dog

David's dog Cindy is twelve years old. David's parents bought her in the pet shop in King Street when David and Cindy both were still babies. Of course they have become best friends. So the boy got a shock when last June Cindy suddenly didn't eat her food any more. She was lying in a corner of the living-room and looking at the boy with sad eyes. "We must go to the vet* with her, Mum," David said, and his eyes were full of tears. At five o'clock in the afternoon they were sitting in Dr Watson's waiting-room. Some minutes later the doctor examined the animal and asked about her food. When he heard that Cindy sometimes got bones, he told David that this was not good for her because she couldn't eat them. So she had problems with her stomach.

After some days the dog felt much better, and so did David!

* vet = Tierarzt

156 words

Diktatauswertung:

Welche Wörter habe ich falsch geschrieben?

Gegen welche Rechtschreibregel verstoße ich am häufigsten?

Gesamtfehlerzahl: _______

The accident

On Monday night a terrible accident happened in Queen Street. A young moped driver did not see the red traffic lights and crashed into the back of a lorry. He fell off the vehicle and was still lying in the street when the ambulance* arrived. The police made the traffic go around him. Then a woman cried and ran towards the injured boy. It was his mother. A policeman took her by the arm and spoke quietly to her. Another policeman was making a sketch of the accident and was asking the people some questions. Soon the boy was carried into the ambulance and taken to hospital. Later we heard that he was lucky. Only his leg was broken.

* ambulance = Krankenwagen

121 words

Diktatauswertung:

Welche Wörter habe ich falsch geschrieben?

____

____

____

____

____

Gegen welche Rechtschreibregel verstoße ich am häufigsten?

____

Gesamtfehlerzahl: ________

A summer camp

The boys and girls of the youth club in Liverpool Street are talking about this year's holiday camp. They have just decided to go to the west coast. Soon they have made their lists so that everybody knows what he needs.

Three weeks later the nine young people are carrying their luggage* from the station to the camping site. Then, after a long discussion, they find a place for their three tents. For the next two hours they are all busy. Kevin and Mary collect wood for the fire and fetch water. Mark and Sandra wash potatoes and cook the meal. Tom runs to the farm, across the field and asks the farmer's wife for some eggs. She tells him to go to the henhouse to get them.

Late in the evening they are all sitting around a big fire and singing songs while Mark plays his guitar.

* luggage = Gepäck

152 words

Diktatauswertung:

Welche Wörter habe ich falsch geschrieben?

Gegen welche Rechtschreibregel verstoße ich am häufigsten?

Gesamtfehlerzahl:________

Collecting clothes for the poor

When Kevin's family went to church last Sunday, they heard of a plan. Everybody should collect clothes for the poor people in Africa. On their way home, they wondered where their old children's dresses and jeans where. Back home they went upstairs and found a big, black box. They opened it and soon had the greatest fun.

Sarah pulled out the pullover she wore on her first day at school. "Look here, there's still an old chocolate stain*!" Kevin tried on the shorts from their holiday in Italy five years ago. "You look like a sausage, brother!" his sister laughed.

One hour later they had quite a lot of blouses, skirts, and pullovers. "Let's put some toys in the bag, too. I can imagine the poor children are happy about them," said Sarah and took her teddy bear. She kissed it good-bye and gave it to the collection.

* stain = Fleck

155 words

Diktatauswertung:

Welche Wörter habe ich falsch geschrieben?

Gegen welche Rechtschreibregel verstoße ich am häufigsten?

Gesamtfehlerzahl:________

Our world in the future

What will the world be like in fifty years? More and more children are afraid of the future. They think that there won't be wild animals, green fields, or clean lakes and rivers anymore. In the summer people can't lie on the beaches because of the burning sun. The children will play inside, and football matches or sports and games won't take place in the open air. Food won't come from farms or gardens: We will have to eat pills.

Or will there be a better life than today? Just imagine, all the people in the world will live together like a big family. There will be many trees in the towns, and you can have a holiday on the moon. Perhaps people needn't work so long and can enjoy a longer life. There won't be strict teachers anymore, but a pupil will learn in front of a friendly computer!

154 words

Diktatauswertung:

Welche Wörter habe ich falsch geschrieben?

Gegen welche Rechtschreibregel verstoße ich am häufigsten?

Gesamtfehlerzahl: ________

Fire at the zoo

Betty and her brother Dave are walking through the zoo. Suddenly they hear a bell ringing and see a cloud of smoke behind the elephant house. Zoo keepers are running around and shouting. "Keep the paths free for the fire engine!" The two children ask another visitor. "What has happened?" He answers that a man threw a burning cigarette* into a basket, and the paper in it caught fire. Now they can hear the noise of the animals. Excited tigers and elephants, monkeys and lions are all calling for help. It's very difficult to keep them quiet and lead them to a safe place. At last the firemen have put out the flames. But hours later you can still smell the smoke in the air.

* cigarette ['sigəret] evtl. buchstabieren

130 words

Diktatauswertung:

Welche Wörter habe ich falsch geschrieben?

Gegen welche Rechtschreibregel verstoße ich am häufigsten?

Gesamtfehlerzahl: ________

An invitation to Scotland

Dear Birgit,

We still think of the exchange visit last April, when you stayed with us and went to our high school.

Sorry, but I can't come to Germany during Easter because I have to work for my exams. But we want to ask you if you could come to Scotland again in summer. You know we like to do many hobbies together. We can go to the bowling centre, or drive to a pony farm in the Highlands. We haven't seen the traffic museum in Glasgow yet, and I'm sure you want to have another big ice-cream in the shopping centre. If you come, please don't forget your warm parka and jeans. You found it very cold when the Scottish wind was blowing.

I hope your answer to this invitation will be 'yes'.

Say hello to your parents and Michael.

Much love from

Dawn

150 words

Diktatauswertung:

Welche Wörter habe ich falsch geschrieben?

____

____

____

Gegen welche Rechtschreibregel verstoße ich am häufigsten?

____

Gesamtfehlerzahl: ________

A big storm

The radio broadcasts* the news every thirty minutes. A heavy storm was coming up from the west coast. The police were driving along the beach and telling sailors to get out of the water and bring their boats onto the land. Big clouds were building up in the sky, and soon the rain started.

In the camp site some tourists tried to put their things inside their tents. Others took their caravans and cars and left the place in a hurry. After three hours the water was two feet high, and you could see tables, chairs, cookers and bikes lying around, all wet or broken. Men, women, and children were looking for their things or helping their neighbours.

On the next day, when the sun came out, you could see how terrible the camping site looked.

* to broadcast = senden

139 words

Diktatauswertung:

Welche Wörter habe ich falsch geschrieben?

Gegen welche Rechtschreibregel verstoße ich am häufigsten?

Gesamtfehlerzahl:________

C. Lösungen

Aufgabe 1:
1. Germany, August, weeks, September 2. school, Peter, building, King Street, London 3. week's, Christmas 4. Italy, America 5. Pedro, Spanish 6. summer, home, Barcelona 7. Peter's father, British Airways 8. Daddy 9. Italian 10. town, Italy 11. England 12. places, streets, London 13. Buckingham Palace, Queen Elizabeth's

Aufgabe 2:
1. Tony, Mary, Scotland 2. Scottish 3. father, brother, Edinburgh, castle 4. mother, Mummy, America 5. Edinburgh, uncle, Uncle, Aunt 6. Castle Road 7. Easter 8. day, week 9. Monday, castle, Scottish 10. Wednesday, English 11. weekend 12. British Airways 13. Edinburgh, Saturday, April 14. India, Australia

Aufgabe 3:
1. beginning 2. reading, writing 3. sitting, feeding 4. barking, looking 5. swimming, shouting 6. sleeping, feeling 7. listening, eating 8. waiting, going 9. cooking 10. waiting 11. helping, throwing 12. putting 13. shouting

Aufgabe 4:
1. sitting, making 2. raining, hitting 3. ringing 4. shouted, stood, opened 5. stopped, talking, looked 6. offering 7. listened, wanted 8. shutting, looked 9. travel 10. waited, asked 11. showed 12. looked, offered 13. helped 14. ordered

Aufgabe 5:
1. cheaper, cheapest 2. bigger, biggest 3. hotter, hottest 4. colder, coldest 5. cleverer, cleverest 6. flatter, flattest 7. cleaner, cleanest 8. fatter, fattest 9. older, oldest 10. lighter, lightest 11. longer, longest 12. larger, largest 13. shorter, shortest

Aufgabe 6:
1. families, holidays, countries 2. ways 3. monkeys 4. toys, babies, parties, hobbies 5. balconies, cities 6. stories

Aufgabe 7:
1. skiing 2. buying 3. hurrying 4. carrying 5. trying 6. tries, lying 7. says 8. cries, playing 9. says, flies 10. dying

Aufgabe 8:
1. paying, tried 2. flying 3. hurrying, trying, playing 4. worried 5. carried 6. lying 7. dying, played 8. carrying 9. burying

Aufgabe 9:
1. earlier, earliest 2. greyer, greyest 3. dirtier, dirtiest 4. hungrier, hungriest 5. tidier, tidiest 6. noisier, noisiest 7. easier, easiest 8. funnier, funniest 9. lazier, laziest 10. sillier, silliest 11. busier, busiest 12. luckier, luckiest

Aufgabe 10:
1. hungrily 2. easily 3. noisily 4. crazily 5. Luckily 6. happily, busily 7. lazily (Die Adverbien sind z.T. austauschbar)

Aufgabe 11:
1. shining, moved 2. imagined, hoped 3. supposed, used 4. decided 5. having, riding 6. agreed 7. arguing 8. hated 9. dancing 10. moving 11. losing 12. coming 13. used, saved 14. phoned 15. becoming 16. using

Aufgabe 12:
1. argues, is arguing 2. pronounces, is pronouncing 3. uses, is using 4. takes, is taking 5. phones, is phoning

Aufgabe 13:
1. finest, nicest 2. expensively 3. larger 4. later 5. nicer 6. nicely 7. safer 8. safest 9. latest 10. largest 11. hugest

Aufgabe 14:
1. zoos, hippos, kangaroos 2. photos 3. kilos 4. thieves, knives 5. chiefs, potatoes, tomatoes 6. wlves, tobaccos 7. roofs 8. wolves, lives

Aufgabe 15:
1. O'Brians 2. Ireland's 3. people's 4. O'Brians' 5. children's 6. books 7. boys' 8. Patrick's, years 9. Willy's 10. He's 11. parents' 12. friend's 13. He's 14. Dublin's, Sundays 15. men's 16. country's

Aufgabe 16:
1. went, drove, made 2. found, meant, got 3. came, ran, flew 4. left, found, made, brought 5. felt 6. came 7. knew, taught 8. blew, said, threw 9. caught, was, made, slept

Aufgabe 17:
1. driven 2. seen 3. met, showed, chose 4. been, sat, began 5. drew 6. paid, gave 7. thought, felt, said 8. told 9. bought, read 10. lost 11. put, left

Aufgabe 18:
1. been, bean; four, for 2. know, no 3. brake, break 4. road, rode 5. hour, our 6. won, one 7. new, knew 8. red, read 9. wears, Where's 10. write, right 11. here, hear 12. I, eye 13. weak, week 14. two, to, two, too 15. threw, through

Aufgabe 19:
1. hat 2. know 3. hate 4. May 5. mouse 6. plane 7. right

Aufgabe 20:
1. mouth 2. head 3. hear 4. now 5. anything

Aufgabe 21:
1. thick, sick 2. listen, lesson 3. love, laugh 4. pig, big